Around the Home

CONTENTS

© Aladdin Books Ltd 1991

Design David West
Children's Book Design
Designer Flick Killerby
Consultant editor J. Stidworthy
Editor Roger Vlitos
Researcher Emma Krikler
Illustrator Ron Hayward

*First published in
the United States in 1991 by*
Gloucester Press
387 Park Avenue South
New York NY 10016

Printed in Belgium

Library of Congress Cataloging-in-Publication Data

Bender, Lionel.
    Around the home / by Lionel Bender.
        p.   cm. -- (Through the microscope)
    Includes index.
    Summary: Examines, through microscopic photographs of everyday objects, the hidden details of the microscopic world in which we live.
    ISBN 0-531-17348-8
    1. Microscope and microscopy--Pictorial works--Juvenile literature. 2. Microorganisms--Pictorial works--Juvenile literature. [1. Microscope and microscopy. 2. Microorganisms.] I. Title. II. Series.
QH278.B45   1991
502'.8'2--dc20   91-9764   CIP   AC

THROUGH · THE · MICROSCOPE

Around the Home

Lionel Bender

GLOUCESTER PRESS
New York: London: Toronto: Sydney

LOOKING CLOSER

Microscopes and magnifying glasses work by using lenses and light. A lens is usually a thin, circular glass, thicker in the middle, which bends rays of light so that when you look through it an object appears enlarged. A microscope uses several lenses. It will also have a set of adjustments to give you a choice over how much you want to magnify.

When we want to view something under a microscope it must be small enough to fit on a glass slide. This is put on the stage over the mirror and light is reflected through so that the lenses inside can magnify the view for us. But not all microscopes work this way. The greatest detail can be seen with an electron microscope which uses electron beams and electromagnets.

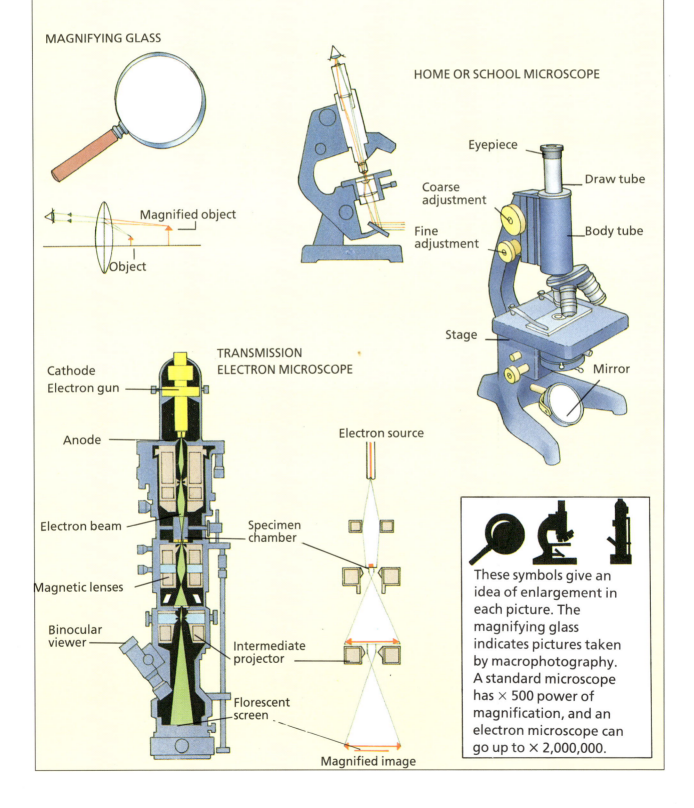

MAGNIFYING GLASS

Magnified object

Object

HOME OR SCHOOL MICROSCOPE

Eyepiece

Draw tube

Coarse adjustment

Body tube

Fine adjustment

Stage

Mirror

TRANSMISSION ELECTRON MICROSCOPE

Cathode
Electron gun

Anode

Electron beam

Magnetic lenses

Binocular viewer

Florescent screen

Specimen chamber

Intermediate projector

Electron source

Magnified image

These symbols give an idea of enlargement in each picture. The magnifying glass indicates pictures taken by macrophotography. A standard microscope has × 500 power of magnification, and an electron microscope can go up to × 2,000,000.

INTRODUCTION

The microscope has played a very important part in our understanding of the everyday world, as well as a key role in the inventions of modern technology. Many everyday objects have been both designed and checked for production quality at a microscopic level. This book contains images of objects that you might find around your house, garage and yard.

These pictures have been taken through microscopes or with closeup lenses on cameras. Next to each picture is a symbol showing by what method each picture was made. This will give you an idea of the number of times objects are magnified compared with life-size. Drawings appear alongside to help explain what the microscopes show.

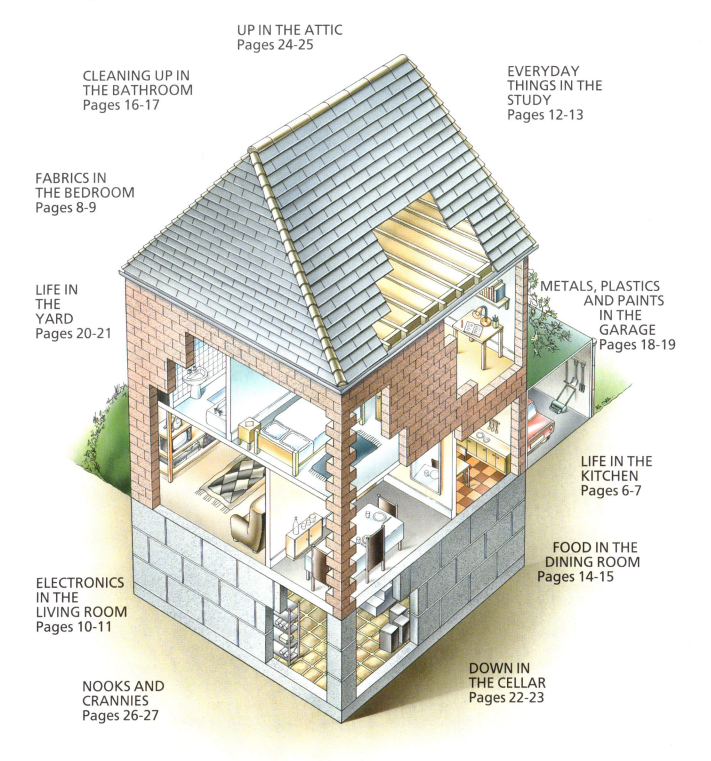

LIFE IN THE KITCHEN

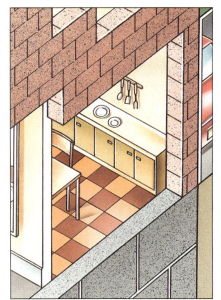

With the invention and use of powerful light microscopes in the 1880s, scientists were able to discover why food rots and how it can sometimes poison us. Both problems are caused by tiny living creatures which are present in even the cleanest of kitchens. Microscopic animals lurk in cracks, on walls, inside closets, and sometimes on food itself. Usually, they do no harm and go about their lives entirely unnoticed by people. Similarly, molds are tiny fungi that release spores which float through the air. They are likely to be present in almost any kitchen, ready to colonize pieces of bread, cheese, or other food that are left lying about. More visible visitors, like common houseflies, often bring harmful bacteria with them.

The photo below (magnified ×2) shows mold on part of a lemon skin. Most fungi consist of branching threads that spread through and over their food, taking in nourishment. But often the most obvious parts of a fungus are the fruiting bodies (sporangia) they send up. These release spores into the air which float away to land on a new food source.

A common housefly

This housefly's head (×50 in the picture above) shows its large compound eyes with many facets. The short antennae that help the fly find food can be seen on the front of the head, with its mouthparts below. It is liable to land on all kinds of foodstuffs to test whether they are suitable to eat. This is a health hazard as flies can carry germs on their feet and mouthparts.

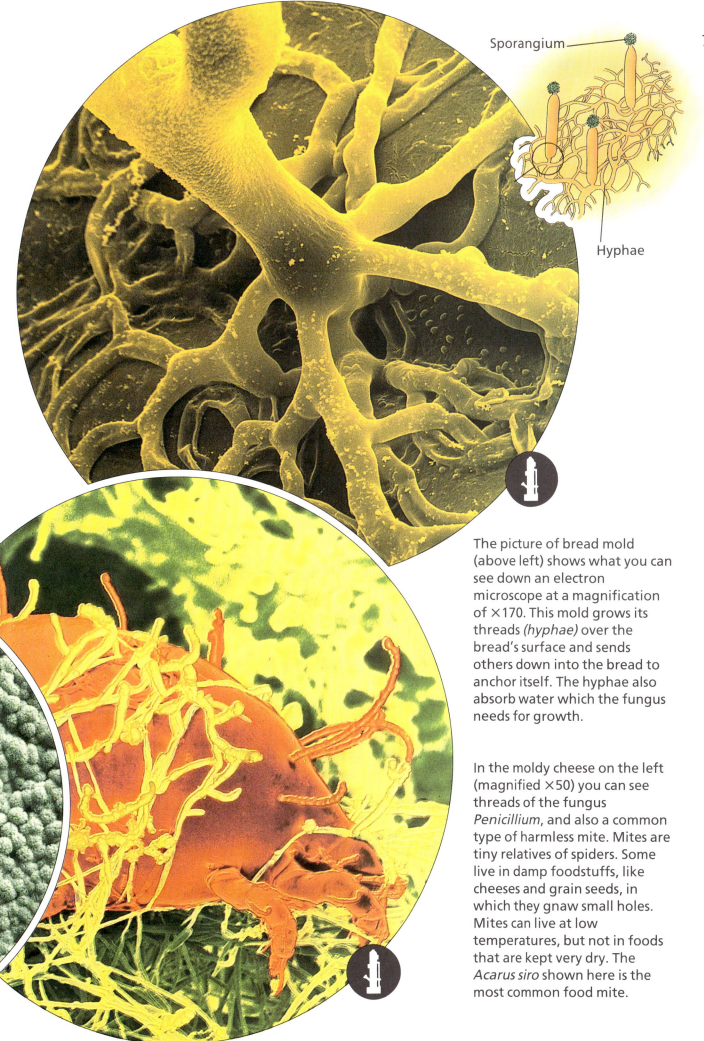

Sporangium

Hyphae

The picture of bread mold (above left) shows what you can see down an electron microscope at a magnification of ×170. This mold grows its threads *(hyphae)* over the bread's surface and sends others down into the bread to anchor itself. The hyphae also absorb water which the fungus needs for growth.

In the moldy cheese on the left (magnified ×50) you can see threads of the fungus *Penicillium*, and also a common type of harmless mite. Mites are tiny relatives of spiders. Some live in damp foodstuffs, like cheeses and grain seeds, in which they gnaw small holes. Mites can live at low temperatures, but not in foods that are kept very dry. The *Acarus siro* shown here is the most common food mite.

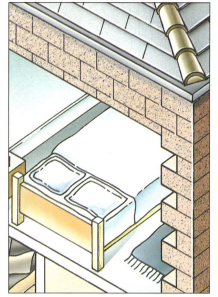

FABRICS IN THE BEDROOM

Fabrics are an essential part of our lives. Clothes keep us warm by day and sheets, blankets and bedspreads do the same at night. Drapes and carpets add to our comfort, while clean towels and linen contribute to our personal hygiene. In general, fabrics are woven from threads or long strands a fraction of a millimeter thick. For example, wool comes from sheep, cotton from the seeds of a bush, rayon from the bark of trees, and the delicate threads of real silk are spun by tiny worms. The microscopic study of natural fibers and fabrics has led to the production of new synthetic ones. These "artificial" fibers are normally much cheaper to produce in the large quantities that modern manufacturers want.

The image (right) shows part of a pair of panty hose magnified ×110. These are made of the artificial fiber, nylon. The yarn for such stockings comes in various thicknesses, the thinnest giving the sheerest stockings when woven. Nylon is a strong fiber, and when woven into a mesh, makes even lightweight stockings reasonably long-lasting. As with many electron microscope images, the color here is not that of the original object, but has been tinted by a computer.

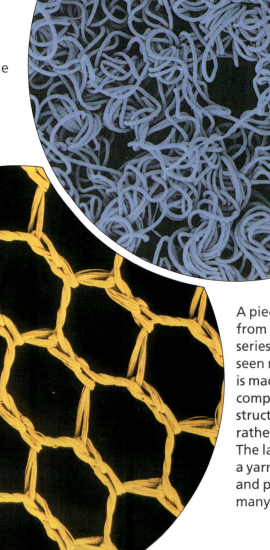

A piece of machine-made lace from a curtain (left) shows a series of very even "cells" as seen magnified ×160. Each cell is made up of a succession of complicated knots, and its even structure is typical of machine- rather than hand-made fabrics. The lace seen here is made from a yarn that includes both cotton and polyester fibers in its many-stranded threads.

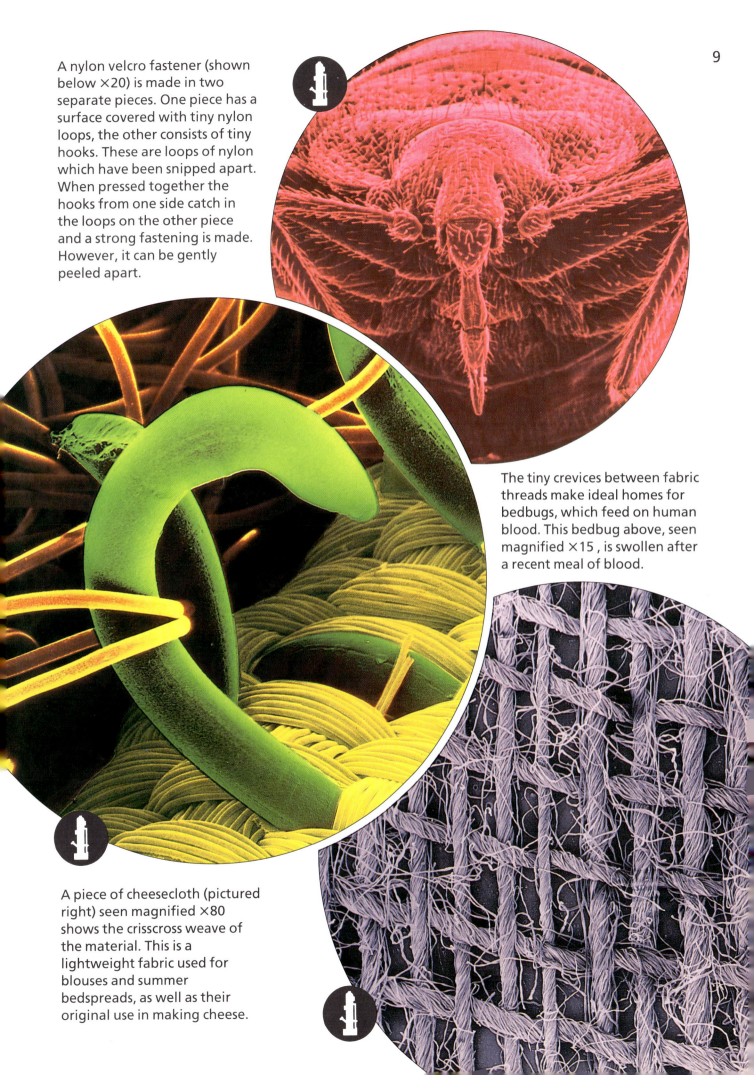

A nylon velcro fastener (shown below ×20) is made in two separate pieces. One piece has a surface covered with tiny nylon loops, the other consists of tiny hooks. These are loops of nylon which have been snipped apart. When pressed together the hooks from one side catch in the loops on the other piece and a strong fastening is made. However, it can be gently peeled apart.

The tiny crevices between fabric threads make ideal homes for bedbugs, which feed on human blood. This bedbug above, seen magnified ×15 , is swollen after a recent meal of blood.

A piece of cheesecloth (pictured right) seen magnified ×80 shows the crisscross weave of the material. This is a lightweight fabric used for blouses and summer bedspreads, as well as their original use in making cheese.

ELECTRONICS IN THE LIVING ROOM

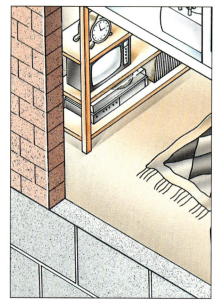

Modern technology has made an ever-increasing range of gadgets and devices available to us today. Many of these items have minute working parts that cannot be seen properly with the unaided eye. This is because they were actually designed and manufactured with the aid of microscopes. On these pages we can see what some of these amazingly intricate structures look like close up. The wires and hand-soldered connections of an electrical circuit used to take up a great deal of space. Today, many thousands of circuits can be fitted into a fraction of the same space within a micro-chip.

Unlike records, the surface of a compact disk (×143 in the picture below) is well protected, and is not worn by playing. A coating of transparent plastic covers the "music." Here the coating is removed to show the playing surface. The flat areas and pits are pressed in the plastic disk and then coated with aluminum which will reflect a laser beam. A sensor reads the flashes made by these reflections and translates them into music.

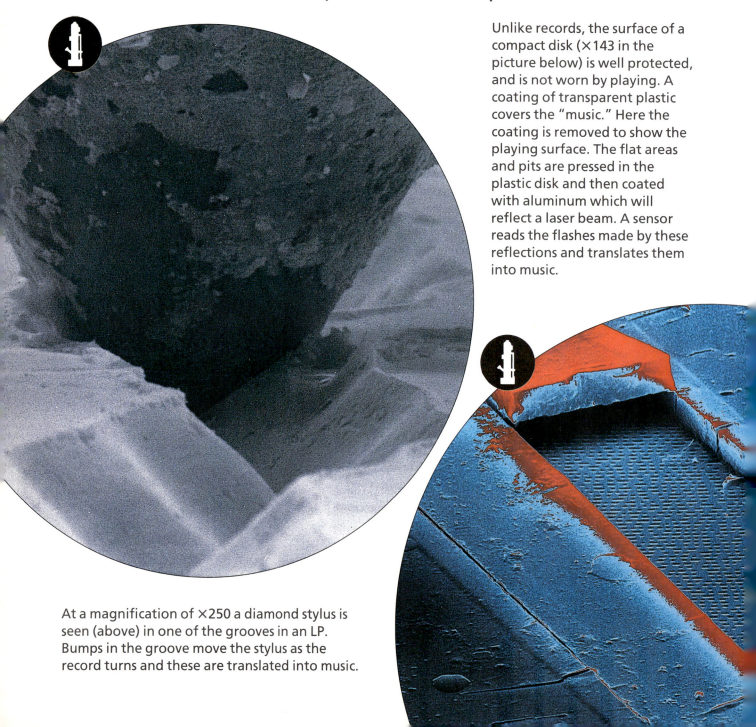

At a magnification of ×250 a diamond stylus is seen (above) in one of the grooves in an LP. Bumps in the groove move the stylus as the record turns and these are translated into music.

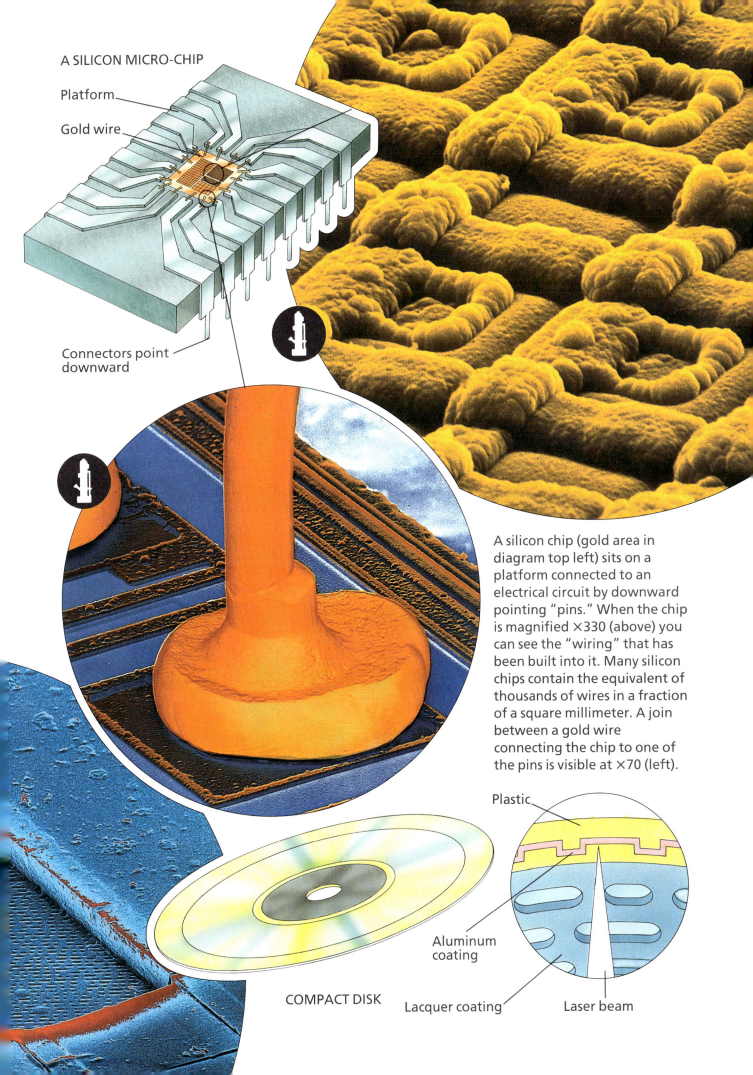

A SILICON MICRO-CHIP

Platform

Gold wire

Connectors point downward

A silicon chip (gold area in diagram top left) sits on a platform connected to an electrical circuit by downward pointing "pins." When the chip is magnified ×330 (above) you can see the "wiring" that has been built into it. Many silicon chips contain the equivalent of thousands of wires in a fraction of a square millimeter. A join between a gold wire connecting the chip to one of the pins is visible at ×70 (left).

Plastic

Aluminum coating

Lacquer coating

Laser beam

COMPACT DISK

EVERYDAY THINGS IN THE STUDY

Under the microscope, common objects such as pens, erasers, elastic bands, clocks, and lightbulbs all show the special aspects of their makeup that can reveal how they work. Papers, for example, differ greatly from one another. The best quality paper is usually found in bank notes. Under a hand lens you can see that there are long and tough-looking strands in it. These are fibers which have been recycled from linen rags. They make the bank note long-lasting and flexible. This means that it can be bent again and again as it passes from hand to hand. A piece of ordinary paper would soon fall apart.

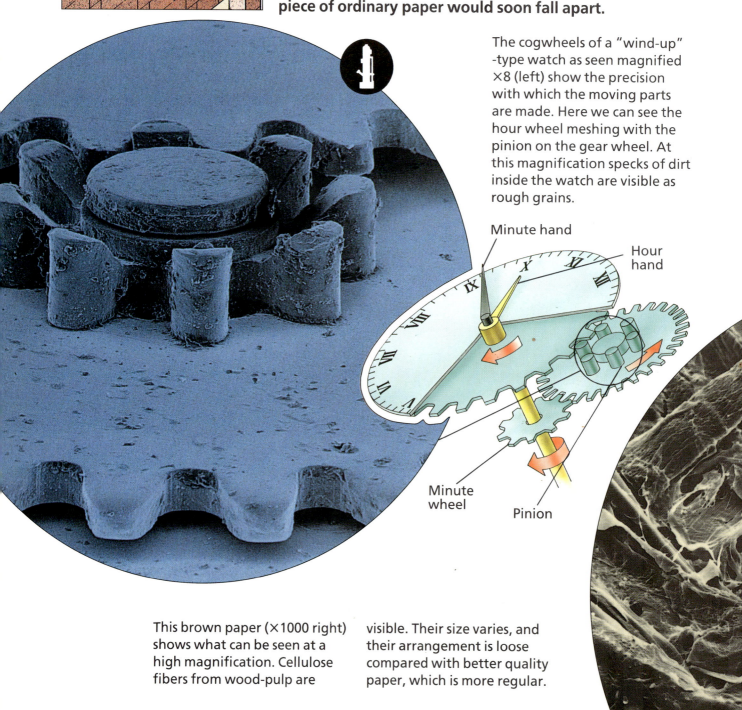

The cogwheels of a "wind-up"-type watch as seen magnified ×8 (left) show the precision with which the moving parts are made. Here we can see the hour wheel meshing with the pinion on the gear wheel. At this magnification specks of dirt inside the watch are visible as rough grains.

Minute hand

Hour hand

Minute wheel

Pinion

This brown paper (×1000 right) shows what can be seen at a high magnification. Cellulose fibers from wood-pulp are visible. Their size varies, and their arrangement is loose compared with better quality paper, which is more regular.

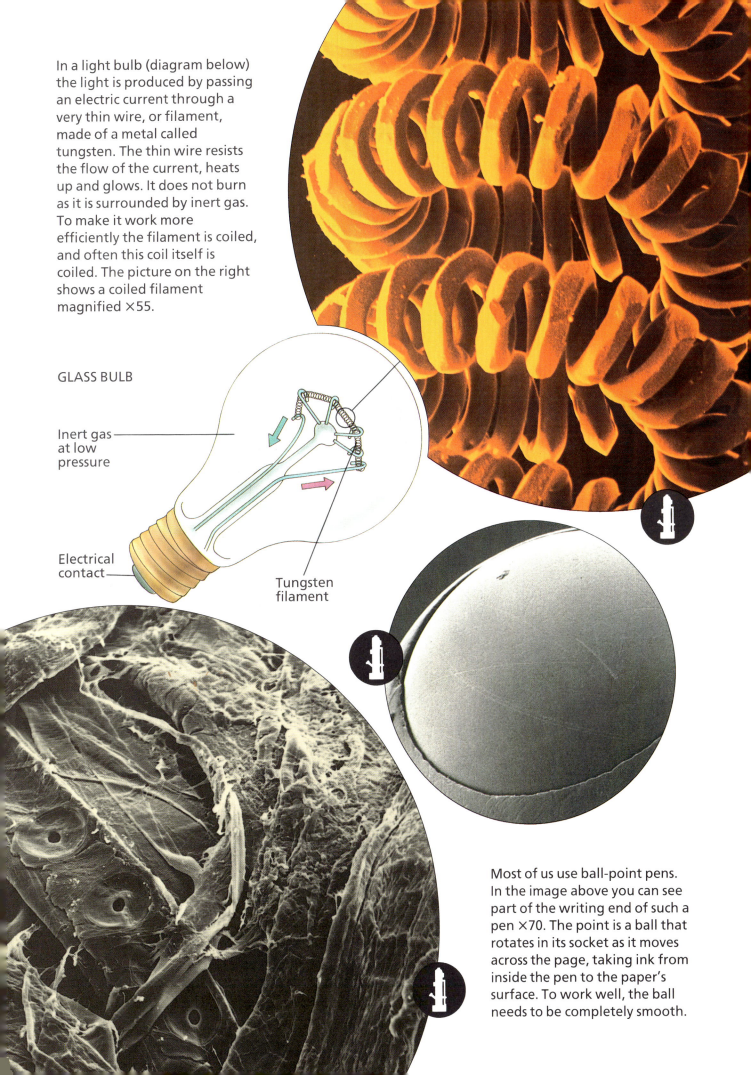

In a light bulb (diagram below) the light is produced by passing an electric current through a very thin wire, or filament, made of a metal called tungsten. The thin wire resists the flow of the current, heats up and glows. It does not burn as it is surrounded by inert gas. To make it work more efficiently the filament is coiled, and often this coil itself is coiled. The picture on the right shows a coiled filament magnified ×55.

GLASS BULB

Inert gas at low pressure

Electrical contact

Tungsten filament

Most of us use ball-point pens. In the image above you can see part of the writing end of such a pen ×70. The point is a ball that rotates in its socket as it moves across the page, taking ink from inside the pen to the paper's surface. To work well, the ball needs to be completely smooth.

14

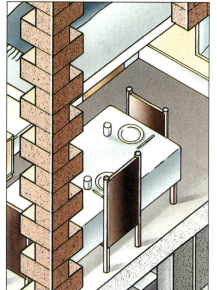

FOOD IN THE DINING ROOM

Microscopic studies have helped nutrionalists, dieticians and food technologists to understand what is important in the things that we eat. As a result we now have a wide range of artificial sweeteners and flavorings, and even meatlike products processed from fungi grown in factory conditions. Most food consists of a mixture of fibers, starch, sugars, fats and water. Cooking makes it tastier, as well as easier to chew and swallow. However, cooking also releases some of the substances within the raw components at the same time as it destroys others. Our bodies can only process and use certain combinations of the food we swallow. There is always much more to food than meets the unaided eye.

Looking at a slice of raw potato (enlarged ×25 below) we can see the regular structure of the cells and egg-shaped grains of starch within. When the potato is cooked (right) the cell walls break down. Notice how the starch inside has turned into a gluey mass.

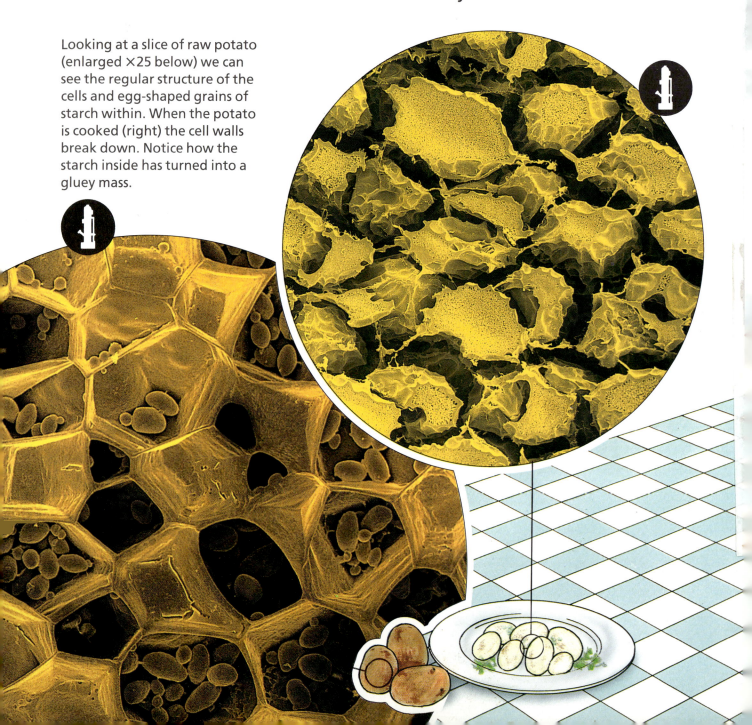

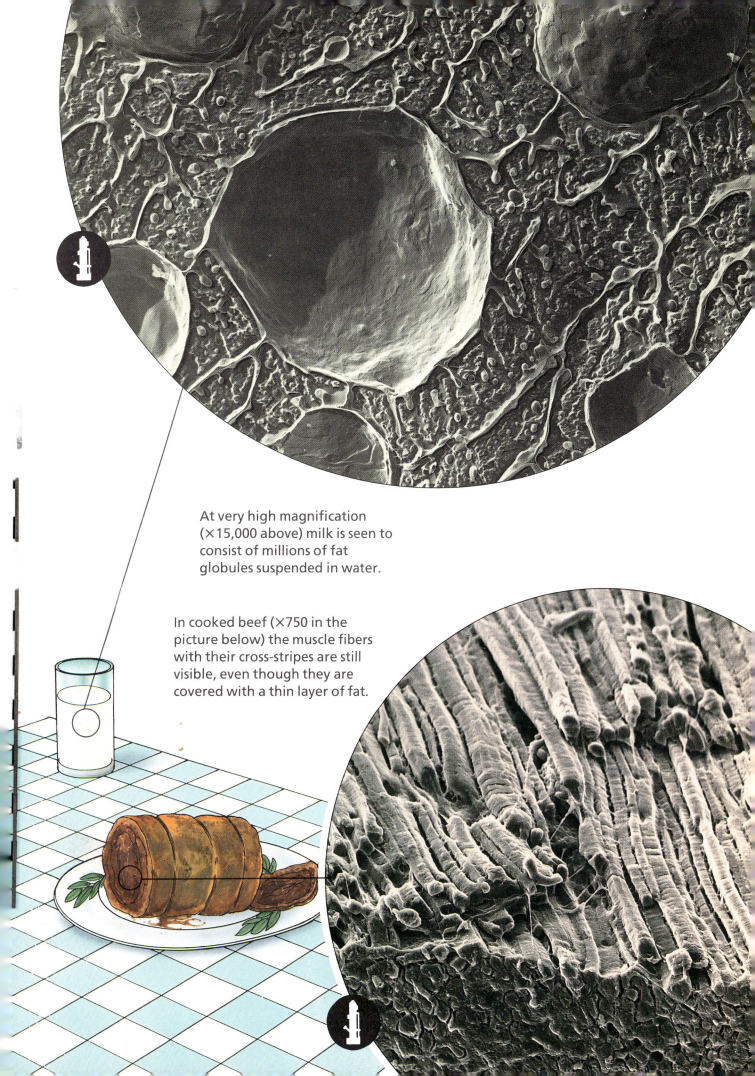

At very high magnification (×15,000 above) milk is seen to consist of millions of fat globules suspended in water.

In cooked beef (×750 in the picture below) the muscle fibers with their cross-stripes are still visible, even though they are covered with a thin layer of fat.

CLEANING UP IN THE BATHROOM

Bathrooms tend to have shiny surfaces of porcelain and tiles that show up dirt and grime and are easy to scrub down. As long as the floor, walls, toilet, sink and tub in a bathroom are regularly cleaned, there is no danger from germs. However, no matter how clean and shiny surfaces look to the unaided eye, microscopic examination shows how much mess we ourselves create. Splashes of water leave behind a residue of chemicals that can harden and become difficult to shift. Flakes of skin and fallen hairs clog combs, brushes, and even drains. Small wonder that some people always seem to be cleaning the bathroom!

A scan of the surface of a bar of soap (magnified ×16 below) reveals a flaky texture that is not apparent to the unaided eye. Used bars such as this accumulate microscopic grit on and between the flakes.

Drops of water are fascinating objects close up. In the image above a tiny water droplet, enlarged ×30, plunges into the surface of some water. The impact of its fall sends plumes of water up all around it. The result is this "coronet" which is visible for a fraction of a second before it collapses back into the water's surface.

An ordinary comb (magnified ×80 right) shows human hair caught up in its teeth. Minute flakes of skin and dirt also stick to the surface. Each of these human hairs is only about 0.02cm in diameter.

The edge of a razor blade (×600 left) shows it is not as smooth as it appears to the unaided eye. Its surface is corroded and has been worn down by use.

18

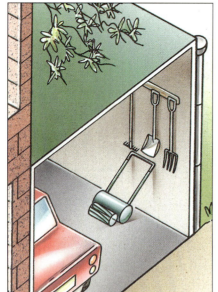

METALS, PLASTICS AND PAINTS IN THE GARAGE

The garage is often home to a host of other items as well as the family car. Many of these are either made of metals that rust or corrode, or have coverings of plastic that eventually harden and crack. The surface of metals and plastics is always interesting when looked at under a microscope. Even the paintwork that covers a car is special and unique to that vehicle when portions of it are viewed microscopically. This has been dramatically proven by forensic scientists who have been able to establish a connection between a car-owner and a crime by matching samples of chipped paintwork.

The joint shown below (×11) has been made with two different metals, aluminum and nickel. Such welds are found on car body panels. They have been welded by rotating the two bars of metal end to end at high speed to produce heat and then forcing the bars together while they are still hot.

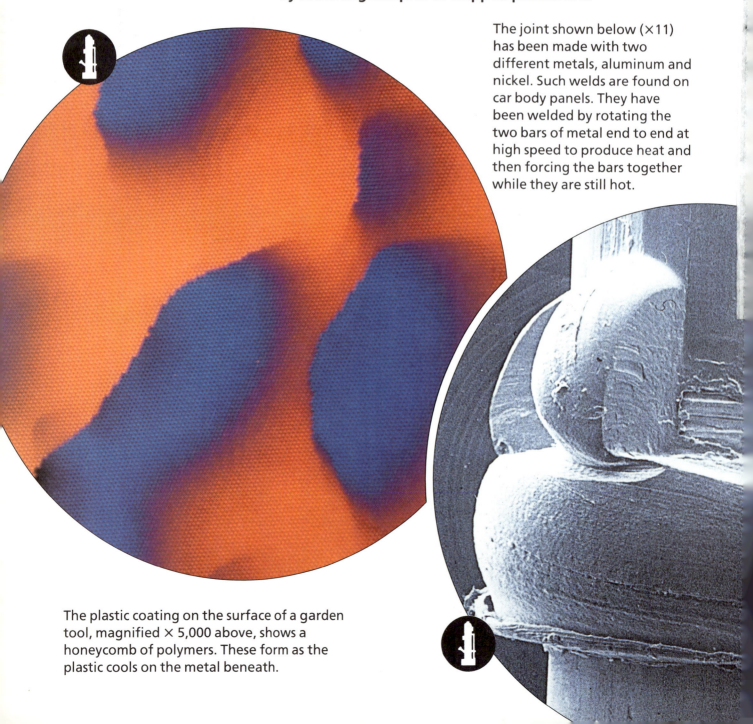

The plastic coating on the surface of a garden tool, magnified × 5,000 above, shows a honeycomb of polymers. These form as the plastic cools on the metal beneath.

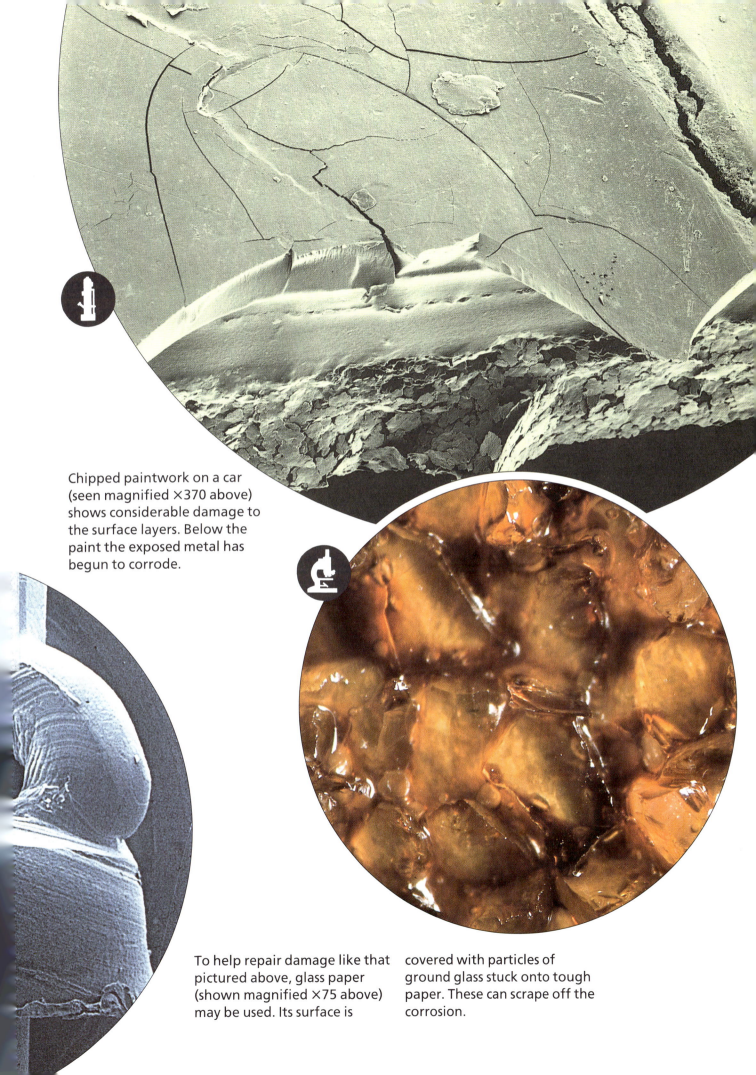

Chipped paintwork on a car (seen magnified ×370 above) shows considerable damage to the surface layers. Below the paint the exposed metal has begun to corrode.

To help repair damage like that pictured above, glass paper (shown magnified ×75 above) may be used. Its surface is covered with particles of ground glass stuck onto tough paper. These can scrape off the corrosion.

LIFE IN THE YARD

Most yards are full of life. Some are easy to see, like the plants growing there and the birds that fly across it. Other living things may be well hidden, or too small to see easily with the unaided eye. Ponds, birdbaths, gutters and the film of moisture around particles of earth can all be home to single-celled creatures and more complex, but still microscopic, life forms. Yards are also full of insects. Some are useful, while others are pests that may damage plants or, like mosquitoes, bite us. A microscope shows details of these creatures that could never be seen with the unaided eye. We can also take sections of plants which reveal the complexities and beauty of their structure, and may also show how they grow and develop.

The head of a biting midge (pictured below ×60) shows the long, sharp proboscis that pierces skin so the midge can suck blood through it. Also visible are the antennae on top of the head and the insect's compound eyes.

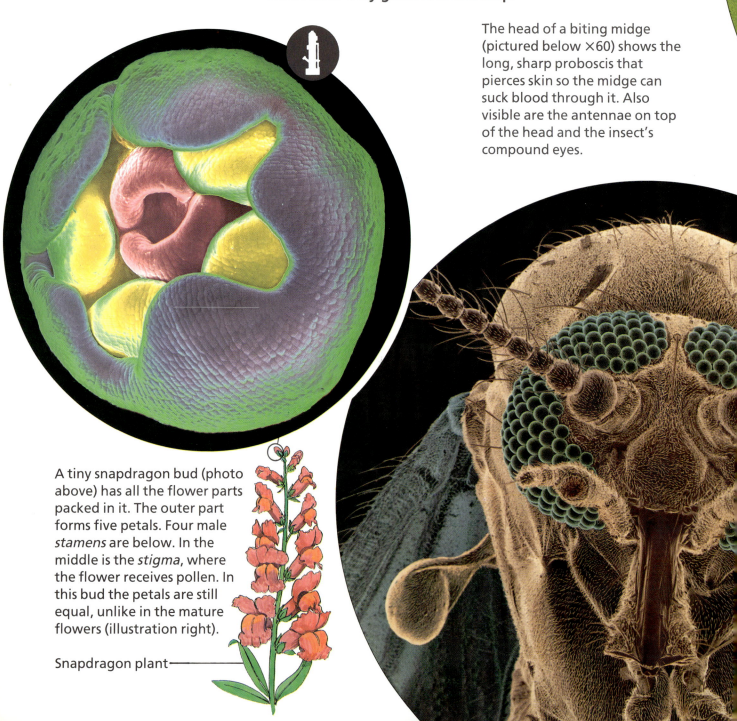

A tiny snapdragon bud (photo above) has all the flower parts packed in it. The outer part forms five petals. Four male *stamens* are below. In the middle is the *stigma*, where the flower receives pollen. In this bud the petals are still equal, unlike in the mature flowers (illustration right).

Snapdragon plant

Ivy

This ivy leaf (×4 left) has begun to rot away leaving the tougher parts, its "skeleton," behind. This is the network of tubes that carry water from the roots to the leaf and sugars from the leaf to the rest of the plant. These tubes are made from plant cells that have a tough chemical called *lignin* in their woody walls.

A sun-animalcule (see below) is a single-celled animal related to amoeba. Its round body is enclosed within a protective silica case with long spines. It lives in water, feeding on bacteria and other tiny animals. This kind is about 0.005cm across and is just visible under an ordinary hand lens.

A midge

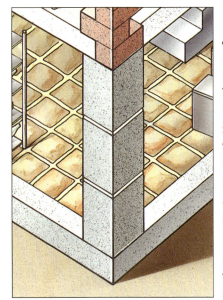

DOWN IN THE CELLAR

Most people rarely take a good look at their cellars. If they did they might not be too pleased by what they saw. Down in the damp all kinds of animals, from woodlice to spiders, are living. In some cellars it may be so damp that woodwork is decaying, infected with fungus. Harder materials, such as brick and concrete, can also decay. They begin to crack as they get older. Stresses and strains caused by damp or frost leave their marks. Even new building materials that look solid to us may look much less so under the microscope. Most bricks , for example, have a honeycomb appearance under the microscope. The tiny spaces fill with air, which helps to prevent cold from getting in and heat from escaping.

A woodlouse (magnified × 55 in the picture below) likes damp, dark places like cellars. It might feed on a pile of old, moldy newspapers stored there.

The picture on the right shows an old brick magnified ×7,425. There are gaps in the baked clay and it is beginning to crumble.

A wide variety of things were found in the dust from a vacuum cleaner (photo right ×60) which was used to clean a cellar floor. We can see building materials such as sand and grit, some synthetic fibers, cat fur, flakes of skin, a few flea droppings, sawdust and insect remains.

Each type of building stone (×500 below) has its own special characteristics. Some are made of large particles, others consist of very fine grit packed tightly together in the stone.

UP IN THE ATTIC

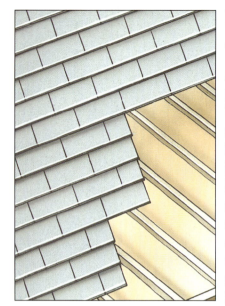

Another forgotten corner of the house is the attic, which may be rarely visited by the house's human inhabitants. There are materials here that are seldom seen in the rest of the house, such as the rock wool or fiberglass used to insulate the loft. There may also be wildlife in the attic. Birds may make their nests under the eaves and bats can live in the rafters or under the roof tiles. These animals always have others living on them. Other visitors may spell danger to the roof. A number of beetles feed on dead wood and will weaken unprotected rafters. They lay their eggs in the wood and the larvae (young) that hatch eat it. Some bore tunnels and may weaken timbers. A few kinds will eventually turn the wood to powder.

The death-watch beetle (×30 below) mainly attacks oak timbers. The larvae may take up to 10 years to develop into beetles. Then they gnaw their way out of their tunnels to the surface.

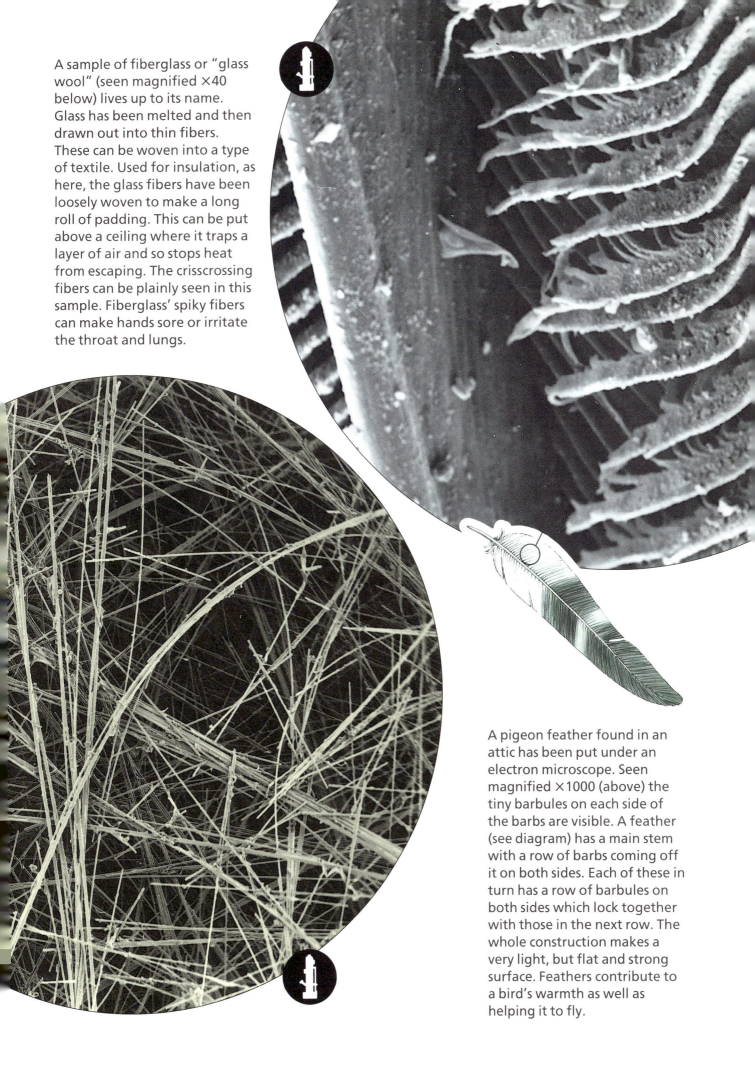

A sample of fiberglass or "glass wool" (seen magnified ×40 below) lives up to its name. Glass has been melted and then drawn out into thin fibers. These can be woven into a type of textile. Used for insulation, as here, the glass fibers have been loosely woven to make a long roll of padding. This can be put above a ceiling where it traps a layer of air and so stops heat from escaping. The crisscrossing fibers can be plainly seen in this sample. Fiberglass' spiky fibers can make hands sore or irritate the throat and lungs.

A pigeon feather found in an attic has been put under an electron microscope. Seen magnified ×1000 (above) the tiny barbules on each side of the barbs are visible. A feather (see diagram) has a main stem with a row of barbs coming off it on both sides. Each of these in turn has a row of barbules on both sides which lock together with those in the next row. The whole construction makes a very light, but flat and strong surface. Feathers contribute to a bird's warmth as well as helping it to fly.

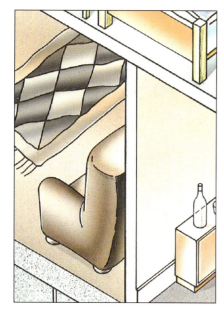

NOOKS AND CRANNIES

In the rugs, behind the furniture, around the window frames – these are just some of the good living spaces we create for small animals that move in and share our homes. If they are not disturbed too often and are not too dry, many tiny animals can live very comfortably in our houses. Many of course, like the spider on the windowsill, are living much as they would if the house was not there. Others are very much dependent on the human inhabitants. For example, the mice that feed on our food would have a much harder time without people. Some animals, of course, feed directly on us. Fleas and bedbugs live in our houses and may suck our blood. Microscopic mites live on us in the pores of our skin.

Some spiders make complicated orb webs (left). Others hunt by springing on their prey. All have fangs that can inject poison. On the spider's head (×6 below) its fangs can be seen below the eyes. Also visible are two clublike organs called *pedipalps*. These are feelers, and are used by adult males in their elaborate courtship and mating ceremonies.

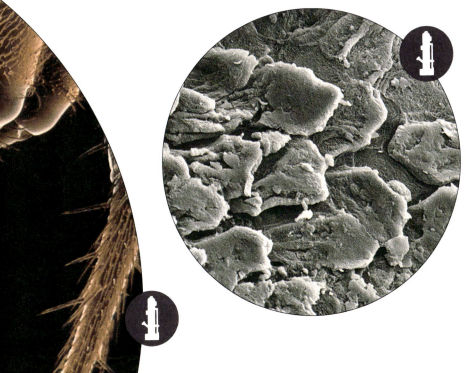

In a pile of household dust (magnified ×800 above) sits a harmless dust mite. These minute animals are found all over the house. They feed on flakes of skin shed by us. A single bed may hold as many as a million mites.

Are these yours? (photo left). This is part of the sole of a human foot as seen when magnified ×750. The surface is covered in flattened overlapping cells. New cells grow from deeper in the skin. As they move nearer the surface they are flattened. These cells are on the ridges and grooves on the sole of the foot.

PRACTICAL PROJECTS

You can discover a great deal about how scientists work with just a hand lens. But to see greater detail you will need a home microscope like that shown on page 4. The objects you wish to study must be mounted on a glass slide. They must be made thin so that light can shine through them. You may need to cut very thin slices of material or to tease them out until they are very fine. To pick out different types of structures, you will need to stain your specimens. The way to do this is outlined below. If you are going to try something that is a bit tricky, it is worth getting help from an adult. You may be able to start your studies with some ready-made slides bought from a microscope supplier.

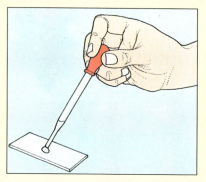

To prepare a cell slide, place a drop of clean water containing the cells on the glass.

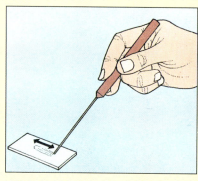

With a wire loop that has been sterilized in a flame spread the fluid thinly and let it dry.

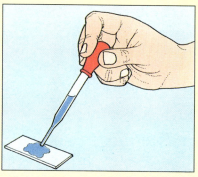

Add a small drop of staining dye to the cells and leave for a few minutes.

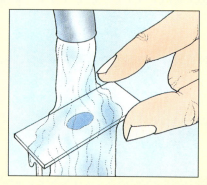

Wash off the dye with water or alcohol. You can stain with another, contrasting dye.

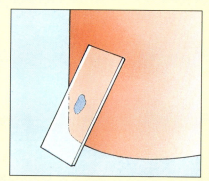

Leave the slide to dry. You can speed up drying by gently warming the slide over a flame.

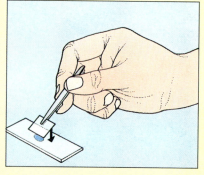

Stick a cover slip (a thin square of glass) over the stained cells, using a pair of tweezers.

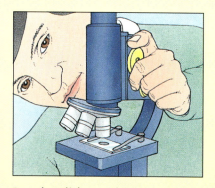

Put the slide on the microscope stage and position the mirror to give you good illumination.

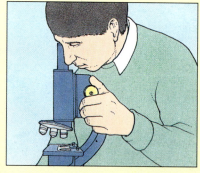

Select the objective lens you want, then move the eyepiece up and down to focus. Start at the lowest magnification.

Keep your prepared slides in a wallet, made from a folded sheet of thin cardboard, which will protect them from dust.

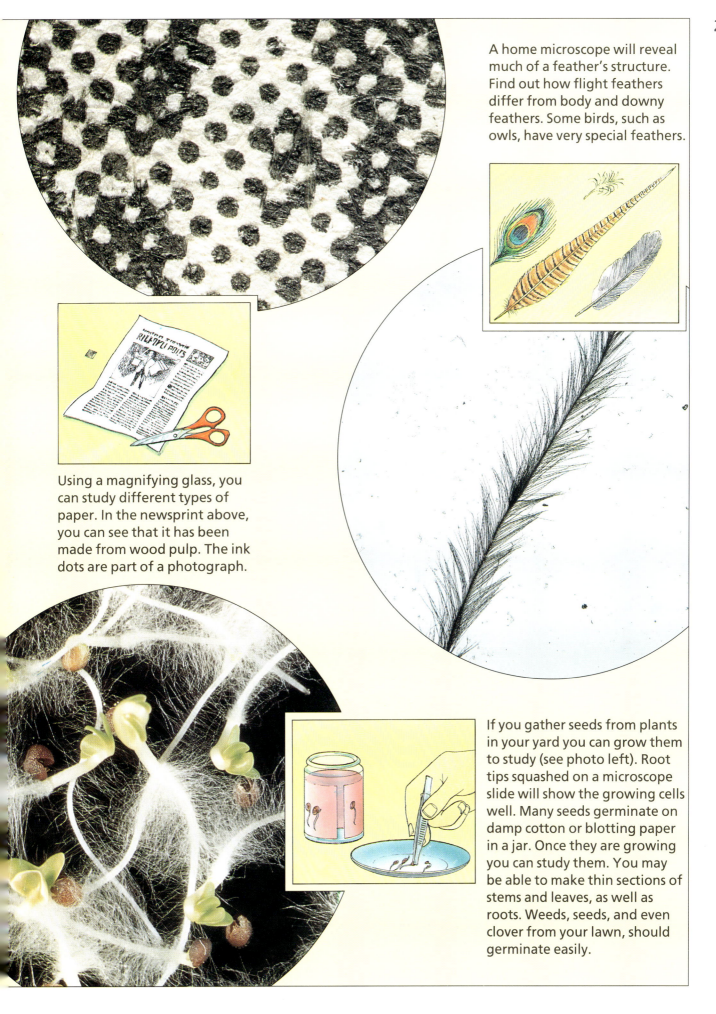

A home microscope will reveal much of a feather's structure. Find out how flight feathers differ from body and downy feathers. Some birds, such as owls, have very special feathers.

Using a magnifying glass, you can study different types of paper. In the newsprint above, you can see that it has been made from wood pulp. The ink dots are part of a photograph.

If you gather seeds from plants in your yard you can grow them to study (see photo left). Root tips squashed on a microscope slide will show the growing cells well. Many seeds germinate on damp cotton or blotting paper in a jar. Once they are growing you can study them. You may be able to make thin sections of stems and leaves, as well as roots. Weeds, seeds, and even clover from your lawn, should germinate easily.

MICROPHOTOGRAPHY

Some of the photographs in this book were taken using a camera with special closeup lenses that magnify the subject in much the same way as a hand lens would magnify them for your eye. Others, with greater magnifications, like the sun-animalcule on page 21, were taken by fitting a camera to the eyepiece of a scientific microscope. Such images are known as photomicrographs. The colors in these are often those of stains used, rather than natural colors. If you have a home microscope you can take your own photomicrographs. You will need a single lens reflex camera and a special camera attachment. Many images in this book were produced using scanning electron microscopes.

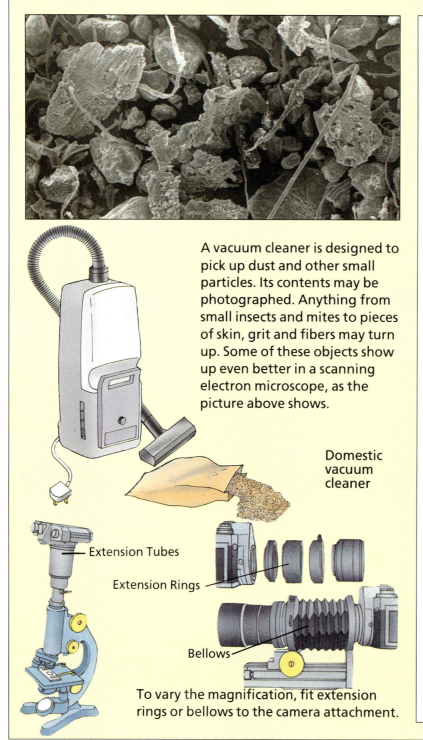

A vacuum cleaner is designed to pick up dust and other small particles. Its contents may be photographed. Anything from small insects and mites to pieces of skin, grit and fibers may turn up. Some of these objects show up even better in a scanning electron microscope, as the picture above shows.

Domestic vacuum cleaner

Extension Tubes

Extension Rings

Bellows

To vary the magnification, fit extension rings or bellows to the camera attachment.

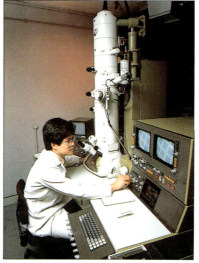

There are two main types of electron microscope. In a transmission type (TEM), a beam of electrons is passed through an extremely thin slice of tissue and an image is produced on a viewing screen. On a scanning electron microscope (SEM), a fine beam of electrons is moved across the surface of the tissue for reflections to be collected and used to create an image on a television type of screen. Using an SEM, realistic 3-D images are produced and, unlike many types of microscope specimens, the creatures can be viewed alive. The normal slide preparation process kills live cells. The photos from an SEM have false colors added in processing.

GLOSSARY

alloy a mixture of metals or a metal with a small amount of nonmetal mixed in.

bacteria a group of simple single-celled microscopic organisms. They are found almost everywhere on earth. Some kinds produce diseases in plants or animals.

cast to make an object by pouring a liquid, molten metal for example, into a mold.

cellulose the substance from which plant cell walls are formed and the raw material of paper. It is also used to make cellulose lacquers for painting.

compound eye type of eye found in many insects, made up of many units or facets.

corrode to rot, break down, oxidize or lose its structure.

facets the units from which a compound eye is formed.

hyphae the threads that make up the main body of many fungi. They may be visible or run underground. Although there may be many meters of these threads, the part of the fungus we usually notice is the fruiting body.

inert not reacting chemically with another substance. Producing no reaction.

insulation a means for preventing heat escaping from (or entering) a room or animal's body.

laser a source of intense pure light of a single color. Laser stands for *light amplification by stimulated emission of radiation*.

molds fungi that produce a network of hyphae visible on the surface of their food, such as those that attack bread and fruit.

natural fiber a fiber such as wool, cotton or silk, produced by animals or plants.

pedipalps a spider's feelers.

polymer a substance that contains very large molecules, each composed of small molecules linked together.

proboscis a trunklike nose, or, in insects, sucking tubular mouthparts.

segmented divided into many separate similar parts.

sporangia hollow, round structures in which fungi produce their spores.

stamens the male parts of a flower. Pollen is produced in the anthers at the top of the stamens.

stigma the sticky tip on top of the female part of a flower (the carpel) that receives pollen.

synthetic fiber a fiber made of polyester, nylon or other artificial substance.

tissue a collection of similar cells in an animal or plant that has a recognizable common function, such as muscle or blood.

tungsten a hard gray metal used as a wire in electric lamps.

welded joined together using heat. Metals and plastics can be welded.

WEIGHTS AND MEASURES

mm = millimeter 10mm = 1cm = 0.4 inch
cm = centimeter 100cm = 1m = 3.3 feet
m = meter 1000m = 1km = 0.6 mile
km = kilometer
lb = pound

g = gram 1000g = 1kg = 2lb 3oz
kg = kilogram
0.1 = 1/10
0.01 = 1/100
0.001 = 1/1000

INDEX

Photographic Credits:
Cover and title page: Science Photo Library; page 6 left: Biophoto Associates; page 6 right and all pages up to and including 12: Science Photo Library; page 12-13: Biophoto Associates; pages 13 top and bottom, 14 top and bottom: Science Photo Library; page 15 top: Bio Associates; pages 15 bottom, 16 left and right: Science Photo Library; page 17 top and bottom: Biophoto Associates; page 18 and 18-19: Science Photo Library; page 19 top and bottom: Biophoto Associates; pages 20, 21 top and bottom, 22, 23 all and 24: Science Photo Library; page 25 top and bottom: Biophoto Associates; pages 26 top and bottom, 27 top and bottom, 29 top and bottom: Science Photo Library; page 29 middle: Geoscience Features.